Looking, Longing and Living

Readying Ourselves for Advent

Regent College 2007 Advent Reader
Edited by Susan M. Fisher

REGENT COLLEGE PUBLISHING
Vancouver, British Columbia

Looking, Longing and Living:
Readying Ourselves for Advent
Copyright © 2007 Susan M. Fisher

Published 2007 by Regent College Publishing
5800 University Boulevard, Vancouver, BC V6T 2E4 Canada
Web: www.regentpublishing.com
E-mail: info@regentpublishing.com

Regent College Publishing is an imprint of the Regent Bookstore
<www.regentbookstore.com>. Views expressed in works published by Regent
College Publishing are those of the author and do not necessarily represent the
official position of Regent College <www.regent-college.edu>.

Library and Archives Canada Cataloguing in Publication

Looking, longing and living: Readying Ourselves for Advent / edited
by Susan M. Fisher.

ISBN 978-1-57383-416-2

1. Christmas–Meditations. 2. Advent–Meditations. I. Fisher, Susan M., 1965-

BV40.L66 2007   242'.33   C2007-906792-1

CONTENTS

Acknowledgments

*T*he response from the wider Regent community to last year's Advent Reader—our first—was so encouraging, and at times overwhelming, that I was nervous about attempting another this year. How could we ever match last year's content and quality? As I have read through this book, all fear is gone!

To our forty-seven writers, a heart-felt thank you for reflecting so deeply and personally on the biblical texts and for composing such beautiful works that I know will be a blessing to many. I am delighted that this collection displays your giftedness with words, the uniqueness of your personalities, and the diversity that is so characteristic of the Regent community.

I gratefully acknowledge the important contributions of those who made this Advent Reader a reality. To Deanna Edsall, thank you for serving as the contact person for our writers' assignments and for offering administrative support. To Mary Romero, our copy editor, thank you for your careful and diligent work in reviewing the submissions. To Rosi Petkova, Regent's brilliant graphic artist, thank you for making everything this College produces look so professional and beautiful. To Dal Schindell, the Director of our Publications department, as with last year's cover, you have once again selected very appropriate and attractive artwork. To Rob Clements of Regent Publishing, thank you again for taking our work and producing this amazing book.

And lastly, I wish to acknowledge the wonderful support of three dear colleagues. To Darrell Johnson, thank you again for the guiding vision and for the Introduction that sets the table for what follows. To Bob Derrenbacker, thank you for assisting in the selection of the passages and for helping me think through the weekly and daily ordering of the texts; your appreciation for and knowledge of liturgy is matched by your servant-like attitude, and for that I am very grateful. And lastly, I wish to thank the woman who gave excellent oversight to this project—my brilliant editor, Susan Fisher. Last year, you came on board to assist me in the editing process and proved yourself to be so valuable and trustworthy that I was able to place the entire job in your capable hands. This year's Advent Reader is wonderful, Susan, and you have done a fabulous job. Thank you.

Richard Thompson
Director of Development,
Regent College
Regent Alum (ThM, 2000)

Introduction

*T*here simply is no other time of the year like the season of Advent. I need only hear or see the word—"Advent"—and I see candles burning, I smell pastries baking, and I hear some of the most exquisite music ever composed. Oh, Advent!

Advent is one of the many seasons of what is commonly called the "Christian Year." Early in the church's history, believers began to look at the whole year through the lens of Jesus' life and ministry. They wanted the rhythm of the year to be shaped not by the rhythms of work and culture, but by the Gospel. Building on the annual celebration of Passover by the Jews—in March or April depending on the movements of the moon—and on the annual celebration of the victory of light over darkness celebrated by the Romans at the feast of Saturnalias on December 25th, they looked at the whole year through the words and deeds of Jesus, the Passover Lamb and Light of the World.

For believers, the year begins with Advent, the season encompassing the four Sundays before Christmas. The year moves into Christmastide, celebrating again and again the wonder of the Incarnation. It keeps moving into Epiphany, focusing on Jesus' baptism, temptation, announcement of the coming of the Kingdom, his teaching and healing ministries. Time naturally moves into Lent, which begins five Sundays before Holy Week, when we are drawn to the servant life of Jesus and the implications for our discipleship—dying to live. Then comes the week that changed the world, Holy Week: Palm Sunday, Maundy Thursday, Good Friday, and Easter Sunday. Each year, we are taken into the mystery of Jesus' death and resurrection. Easter continues through Ascension Day up to Pentecost, which arrives fifty days after Easter, when we remember that life in Jesus is life filled with and animated by the Holy Spirit. This season continues through the summer and fall, culminating on the last Sunday of the Church year, Christ the King Sunday, which is usually the third Sunday of November. This day we celebrate the good news that the Bethlehem Child sits on the throne of the universe and nothing can stand in the way of the coming of his Kingdom.

Advent is, for me, the richest season of all because of the texts we read, texts that nurture longing and waiting. Each Sunday of Advent believers light a new candle during the Lord's Day worship. Different traditions give different names to these four candles. Some call them the Angel's Candle, the Mary Candle, the Joseph Candle and the Shepherd's Candle. Others focus more on Christ himself, and have the Prophet, Priest, King and Saviour Candles; or candles for the titles Son of Abraham, Son of David, Son of God and Son of Man. Yet another tradition assigns the themes of Hope, Peace, Love and Joy to the four Sundays of Advent. While we asked our writers to be aware of these latter weekly themes, naturally,

1

the word itself and the Holy Spirit at work in their hearts and lives guided their responses to the biblical text.

We encourage you each morning and each evening to light a candle, read the biblical text, read the reflection on the text, and then spend time in prayer response.

A blessed Advent to you and those you love. In the name of him who came, comes, and is coming.

Darrell W. Johnson
Associate Professor of Pastoral Theology
Regent College

Isaiah 2:1-5

Let the Story Begin!

The stage is set, the curtain about to be drawn. In the theatre of would-be-restored creation the audience stirs in their seats.

We pine as lovers, awaiting God's redemption story to burst into our fallen world—overtaking and rewriting our own sin-spoiled narratives. Nevertheless, a dark fear lies in our hearts. That crucial question we nearly dare not ask: Will it work? Everything is riding on this. Christ is our only hope. If he overcomes, we overcome. If he fails, we fail—everything fails.

We can't fathom the extent of it, but the obstacles are enormous. All hell will come against him. Evil kings who kill infants, religious authorities crying, "Blasphemy," mobs exchanging "Hosannas" for shouts of "Crucify him!" But still larger looms the Curse. The Curse that has gripped us all, since Adam, with a strangling claw. Can sin be stopped? Can evil be routed? Is there a death blow to knock out Death itself?

Isaiah answers. Before the opening credits roll he says not "if" or "when" but "will." God's Christ will prevail. This blessed assurance leaps off the pages of the scroll: "The Lord's temple will be established, it will be raised. Peoples will come. He will teach us his ways. The law will go out, he will settle disputes. Men will beat their swords into plowshares, nations will train for war no more."

Yes, Isaiah! Yes, our God! Let the story begin! Our story, and creation's story —for we are grafted into the story of Jesus Christ!

Come, let us walk in the light of the Lord.

Richard Braaksma
Venice, CA
Writer, Pastor, Coffeehouse Proprietor
Regent Alum (MDiv, 1998)

Matthew 24:36-44

God-Grounded Hope

ut about that day or hour no one knows, not even the angels in heaven, nor the Son, but only the Father.

We aren't very good at "not knowing." We want to know the time, the day, the place. We want all the details, the comprehensive explanation, the airtight case, the inescapable logic. When we seek that kind of knowing for the future, we end up with a "hope without eschatology." Such hope may claim a future that is clearly revealed by the trajectory of history. Or a future that we have been able to guarantee through social planning, or technological innovation, or political savvy. But such hope that depends upon anything in this present age is no hope.

To be plausible, such hopeless hope depends upon ignorance of the world's suffering, unrealistic optimism about the future, implausible confidence in human mastery of life, or the anesthetizing effects of narcissistic pleasure. Jesus offers us hope grounded solely in God. Nothing, no one else. This hope depends upon the shocking irruption of God's redemptive work in creation and in Israel which climaxes in the advent of the Messiah who gives the Spirit to the church.

God-grounded hope knows that when God's peace and righteousness come to this world, they come with judgment, as in the days of Noah. Such hope mourns the evils of this age, prays to God for forgiveness, knows the poverty of our own power, and hungers and thirsts for the kingdom. Such hope lives by the vision of God setting things right in the new creation. By living in this way of hope, we remain ready for the coming of the Son of Man.

Jonathan R. Wilson
Pioneer McDonald Professor of Theology,
Carey Theological College
Regent Alum (MCS, 1980; MDiv, 1985)

Genesis 2:4-25

Beauty Matters

Christ was born into a world of suffering, darkness, fragility, and alienation. Contrast Adam, who was welcomed into a world of beauty, fecundity and the prodigal love of God. Any primitive lover-of-tales would read the garden's topography like a text: ...the garden at the mouth of four rivers which flow down? Why – the garden must be on top of a mountain, where God dwells. Humanity's birthplace is into God's own presence and communion. But Adam is immediately given an assignment, and it is this task that completes his humanity. The animals have not been given names: Adam is to enter into that terrifying and awesome responsibility of adding to the beauty. God—you want me to name them? Won't you just tell me what they are supposed to be named? What if I get it wrong? What if I change my mind later on? Adam is to offer the world created for him back to the Creator by reshaping and refiguring it in love.

We know the rest of the story. We live it day by day, hour by hour. Elizabeth added to the beauty by consoling another person in depression, doubt, confusion. Zechariah added to the beauty by being silent. Mary added to the beauty by giving birth to another human life.

And Christ added to the beauty by himself becoming disfigured, and thus transfiguring all our notions of beauty forever more. Christ—the advent of beauty. Hallelujah.

> All things counter, original, spare, strange;
> Whatever is fickle, freckled (who knows how?)
> With swift, slow; sweet, sour; adazzle, dim;
> He fathers-forth whose beauty is past change:
> Praise him.
> ~ Gerard Manley Hopkins, "Pied Beauty"

Julie Canlis
Methlick, Scotland,
Scotland Children's Spiritual Formation
Regent Alum (MCS, 2000)

Genesis 3

"Where Are You?"

*I*nvitation, colour, excitement, new flavours. The sweet smell of the forbidden. It anticipated for Eve new ways and new relationships. You will be like God! But it was forbidden nonetheless by our loving Creator, because he loved us. This chapter tells us how the human soul was introduced to a dark new model for life—autonomy. How did this happen? When did it begin? So we ask when we are in deep trouble. Rebellion against God is at the core of personal sin and social sin. Eve first, then Adam, had crossed the only boundary God had told them not to cross. Of course, the sweet voice of the serpent lured Eve's heart into desiring what was expressly forbidden. The questions God addressed to Adam did not have the purpose of gathering data; rather, they brought to light the problem of denial, blame, fear and shame. Isn't that the way we often react when we are caught? Behind these reactions there is deep pain, which can only be healed when they are brought to the light, to the truth of God. Having been cast out of the garden and away from the presence of God, humanity, you and I, can only find the path back through Jesus Christ, our LORD and Saviour.

God is still posing this question: "Where are you?"

Jesus took upon himself the consequences and pain of our selfish decisions long before you and I were born. Let us bring to him our pain, our rebellion, our sorrow. May his resurrection power lift us up in joy and hope.

LORD, as I prepare my heart for this season, I confess that at times I fall into denial of my true condition. You remind me today that I need a Saviour. I don't want to hide in shame any longer. Thank you for sending my LORD Jesus.

Ana Maria Cardenas
Quito, Ecuador
Pastor and Economist
Regent Alum (DipCS, MCS, 1993)

Genesis 12:1-9

So Much Greater

A friend of mine recently celebrated sixty years of ministry and preaching. For many of those years he was a missionary in the Congo, then returning to the UK after Congo's independence. He had a clear call from God to go to the Congo when he was just twenty and like Abraham was obedient to his call. "God," he said, "had given him everything he needed," including—to his surprise —languages.

My friend's life story is a good reminder that doing God's work is nothing new, that we are just a part of the fulfilment of God's great promises to Abraham. We are a part of the everlasting covenant between God and Abraham and all of his descendants for generations to come. As followers of Jesus, we are people living under his promises. Advent is a great time to think about what it means to be his people. It is good to ask ourselves, "Where are we being called to obedience?"; "How or to whom are we a blessing?"; and, "How are we blessed?" It is a time to reflect on God's providence, generosity and faithfulness to us, and the enormous love that he has for all of his creation.

Abraham's call was just the beginning of something so much greater than himself and he could never have known where his obedience would lead. Likewise we have our part to play, as did my friend who went to the Congo. We have no idea what doing our part might mean for the future of God's Kingdom.

> Glory to God, whose sovereign grace
> Hath animated senseless stones;
> Called us to stand before His face,
> And raised us into Abraham's sons!
> ~ Charles Wesley
> "Glory to God, Whose Sovereign Grace."

Sarah Tillett
Vicar of the Benefice of Bloxham, Milcombe and South Newington
Director of Arocha UK and Tearfund
Regent Alum (MCS, 2001)

Genesis 17

Letting God Off the Book

Some of the most astonishing promises that God has ever made to a single human being are recorded in Genesis 17 where, speaking to Abram, God announces: "I will establish my covenant as an everlasting covenant between me and you and your descendents after you for the generations to come, to be your God and the God of your descendents after you."

How does Abraham, our father in faith, respond to being addressed thus by God Almighty?

He laughs. "Yeah, right," he chuckles to himself, "like that's ever going to happen..."

Can we blame him? It had been seventeen years since God had last promised him a son (Gen. 15) and many, many years since he had first been promised that he would become a great nation (Gen. 12). By chapter 17 Abraham is an old man and his wife, Sarah, is far beyond the possibility of conceiving and bearing a child. "If only Ishmael might live under your blessing," Abraham offers, graciously trying to let God off the hook.

Yet less than a year later Sarah did give birth to Isaac; and, the people of Israel did eventually take possession of the land of Canaan. Abraham did become the father of many nations; and all the peoples on earth have, in fact, been blessed through him.

As astonishing—and as unlikely—as God's promises to Abraham were, he made good on each and every one of them.

Does it seem unlikely that God will ever make good on his promises to us? Is it hard to believe that Jesus will ever return to renew our shattered world? Should we let God off the hook by lowering our expectations?

Genesis 17 suggests that even if we do, God will still make good on his astonishing promises to us. Maranatha!

Craig Gay
Professor of Interdisciplinary Studies,
Regent College

Numbers 24:1-19

Our Morning Star

A remarkable story this! Balaam, an Israeli prophet, and his donkey, were caught literally between a rock and hard place by God's angel (though the donkey recognised the messenger and balked, refusing to carry his master forward to curse the people of Israel, which Balak, the Moabite king had induced Balaam to do.)

Balaam, caught between God's will and Balak's will, was pulled in two directions, either to receive the riches and honours promised by Balak, or to follow divine direction and bless Israel and her armies.

Finally Balaam yields to God's Spirit and, in a poetic prophecy, affirms the unique role of God's people, comparing them to flourishing palm groves, river-fed herb gardens, cedar trees, and fertile seedbeds. For a desert people, this was alluring indeed. Balaam declares himself to be one "whose eye is clear," who hears from God, sees the vision, and falls down in reverence before God.

Like many Old Testament prophets, Balaam, once he'd gotten his own self-serving desires out of the way, had 20/20 vision, foretelling history's most pivotal event, "A star shall come out of Jacob, and a sceptre shall rise out of Israel...One out of Israel shall rule."

What hope and anticipation this blessing would raise among the Israeli tribes just beginning to take possession of the Promised Land!

When the Spirit speaks with power, as he did with Balaam, and centuries later with young Mary in Nazareth, hope enters the world like a morning star. Unlike hesitant, conflicted Balaam, Mary immediately offered her virgin self to be the God-bearer, in whom the Messianic prophecy was fulfilled in Jesus.

Can we bring hope to our world, as Jesus, our Morning Star, blazes in our hearts?

Luci Shaw
Author, Writer in Residence, Board of Governors,
Regent College

9

2 Samuel 7:1-17

And Then It Gets Even Better!

The promises began for David in a pasture where God gleaned the least of Jesse's eight sons and promised him what seemed like the world. David probably didn't expect that meant facing down a giant and running from a fickle king. But eventually David rested safe from his enemies, in a palace, on a throne where he stopped and realized he had it better than God. God was still in a tent.

I imagine God smiled and reminded David that his God was dwelling right where he should be, with his people, every step along the journey from humble slavery, through the desert of desolation, to a place of promise, of rootedness, home and safe, free from oppression. And then it got even better.

God promised David an unimaginable future—from his very own body would come the One who would rule as king forever. But with a twist.

This One wouldn't be a David sort of king: a warrior, a murderer, a lover. This king, God's very own heart and home, would be born in a cowshed. He would face down the devil, be pursued to the cross, and crowned king of the Jews. And as glorious as David was, he would always be a servant to the One to come.

In our beginning, he searches for and finds us. In our desolation, he holds us close and helps us to persevere. Hopefully, in our comfort, we stop and realize that the LORD has dwelt with us through the whole of the journey. And then it gets even better—but it may come with a twist.

Duffy Lott Gibb
Coordinator of Arts, Summer School and Events,
Regent College
Regent Alum (MCS, 1998)

Jeremiah 31

I Will

A relationship between the new covenant and the advent of Jesus emerges when *Yahweh's* declaration of it in Jeremiah is cited in Hebrews 8:8-12. The immediate contextual argument around this quotation is that Jesus is our superior High Priest because he is the mediator and guarantor of this superior covenant (7:21-22; 8:6). He could not, however, have fulfilled that role without the assumption of our humanity (2:14-18; 4:14-16). The three elements of the covenant are character transformation: "I will put my law in their minds and write it on their hearts," intimacy with God: "I will be their God, and they will be my people.... they will all know me," and pardon: "I will forgive their wickedness..." Each element depends upon God the Son becoming human.

All three aspects are "I will" statements, signalling the theo-centric nature of this covenant. There is an implied responsive human participation in it, enabled by the Spirit (Ezek. 36:26-7), but the covenant is covenanted by God alone. What further evokes our Advent worship is the vicarious Christological fulfilment of the covenant. The interiorization of the moral law which enables obedience was fulfilled perfectly—and vicariously for all humanity—in the fully human Jesus. He has healed what he assumed. Thus, already justified in him, our transformation is further inspired by his empowering sympathy, acquired through his human experience of temptation and suffering (2:14-18; 5:1-5). Jesus' incarnation was critical to our covenant intimacy with God. We can only know him by the Spirit subjectively, because he first made himself known to us objectively in Christ, as incarnate Son (1:1-3). Pardon for our sins through his "once for all" sacrifice (9:11-10:18) was vicarious only because he was "made like his brothers and sisters" (2:18). It is guaranteed by the endless life of this interceding, Divine-human Priest (7:24-5).

W. Ross Hastings
Associate Professor of Mission Studies,
Regent College

Micah 5:2-5

Lightning Strikes

*I*t was never a town that held much promise. A hick town really. Still, directed by the LORD, the prophet Samuel visited Bethlehem. Replacing the reckless Saul was a high priority. He found David. David, the boy left behind, the shepherd boy, the most unlikely boy in a family of strapping young men. This boy would become the new and great king. David was anointed by Samuel right there in Bethlehem.

Lightning strikes a place once. But twice?

It seemed too much to hope for, but in chapter five of the book of Micah, the prophet offers that very promise to exiled Israel: another great ruler would come from tiny Bethlehem: "…one who is to rule in Israel, whose origin is from old, from ancient days…and he shall stand and feed his flock in the strength of the LORD." By any count, humanly speaking, it was a long shot.

The God of Israel, though, seems strangely drawn to the small and unlikely, and hundreds of years later, out in the darkness at the edge of town, in a stable, a young Jewish girl with a shameful secret, endured painful labour. A new ruler was born. Mary called her boy Jesus.

Lightning struck Bethlehem twice. Call it a second miracle.

The third? The lightning that struck Bethlehem that night still lights up the darkness of our world. Pilgrims still stream into Bethlehem to see the great Church of the Nativity. A star with the Latin inscription, *Hic De Virgine Maria Jesus Christus Natus Est,* "Here Jesus Christ Was Born of the Virgin Mary," marks the place of the manger there. Light stills shines from the star. This Advent season, this very day, we worship a King who is great to the ends of the earth!

Mark Harris
Halifax, NS
Pastor
Regent Alum (MCS, 1991)

Psalm 2

Beware: Messiah Coming!

*I*s Jesus meek and mild? Or is Jesus mean and wild (to quote Mark Galli)? Yes.

Psalm 2 is messianic in theme, admonishing in tone. Beware: Messiah on the loose. Take care: Messiah easily angered. Come as supplicant, or not at all. Put away all mocking and defiance, lest his amusement swiftly turns violent, and he looses twelve legions of angels.

This is no picture of gentle Jesus. This is not an account of the meek inheriting the earth. It is a portrait of the King of kings and LORD of lords, imperial and implacable, demanding nations for his own, ruling them however he sees fit. The humble king riding on a foal is now the warrior king astride a stallion, riding out conquering and to conquer.

Beware: Messiah Coming.

Strange text for Advent. Strange theme to illumine the hope we have in the little child away in a manger.

Yet not so strange.

Is Jesus meek and mild? Or is Jesus mean and wild? Yes.

The hope is precisely both.

The humble Christ, manger-laid, foot-washing, cross-bearing Christ, crucified, is all those things by divine necessity, not human. He was not forced by weakness of temperament or the misfortune of circumstances into menial duties, lowly estates.

It was not as if he had no choice.

It's simply that, in Bethlehem and Galilee and Jerusalem and Calvary, he stooped to conquer.

It won't always be thus. And not only Psalm 2 attests to this: Revelation depicts this Messiah as both the Lamb who was slain and the King who will slay. Psalm 2 (mercifully) alerts us to the latter reality, and warns us to choose now what one day we will have to do anyhow: bow our knee and confess with our tongue that Jesus Christ is LORD.

Blessed are all who take refuge in him.

Mark Buchanan
Duncan, BC
Pastor & Author
Regent Alum (MCS, 1990)

Daniel 7:1-14

Dominion

hen God said, "Let us make man in our image, in our likeness, and let them rule...over all the earth" (Gen. 1:26). In Daniel's dream here in chapter 7, however, government through the ages does not have a human face, but a "beastly" one. The human fate is to suffer animalistic domination, represented here by the four terrifying, mutant beasts that emerge from the great wild sea. This government is often immensely powerful (notice the ten horns of the fourth beast—five times as many as one would expect), and it is often immensely arrogant (notice the "mouth speaking great things" on the eleventh horn). It opposes God and it crushes humanity. Happily, though, God is stronger than this anti-God and will one day act to bring an end to its rule. Daniel sees this also in his dream: the passing of dominion over the earth from the beasts to someone who is "like a son of man" (13), that is, "like a human being" (cf. Ezek. 2:1; Num. 23:19), in contrast to previous government that was "like a lion" and so on. This person comes with the clouds (13—he is divine (for cloud, like fire, is often associated with God's appearing in the Old Testament; cf. Ex. 16:10). Yet he is distinct from the "Ancient of Days" who presides over the court. This mystery is not further elucidated until we reach New Testament times, and we meet the divine Son of the Father, who takes to himself the title "Son of Man" and promises to return to finish the work that Christmas has begun: the bringing in of his kingdom (Mk. 13:21-27).

But when the Son of Man comes, will he find faith on the earth (Luke 18:8)?

Iain Provan
Marshall Sheppard Professor of Biblical Studies,
Regent College

Psalm 72

Prayer for the New King

We don't get the newspapers delivered to our home in Sri Lanka. To read about looming terrorist attacks, kidnappings by paramilitary gangs and police corruption could make you stay permanently indoors. So we simply go to work, and at mid-morning tea break, we sift through the propaganda and sigh through the tragedies with colleagues. How bad does it need to get before things change?

For the covenant-conscious Israelites of each succeeding generation, the descent into chaos and national disintegration must have been bewildering. It shows up even in "celebratory" psalms like Ps. 72, which was probably a coronation hymn originally composed for, or shaped by the memory of, Solomon. Certainly, some of the glories that it envisioned were fulfilled in his reign, such as economic prosperity and international prestige. But in other critical areas such as social justice, Solomon's reign sowed seeds of despair that would rend Israel apart. When the hymn was sung in subsequent generations, it is possible that the lessons of Solomon's ambivalent legacy rang through its words. Without being cynical, the prayer for the new king looks beyond the euphoria of the present to a truer day when someone worthier will take charge and put things right. In its prayerfulness, realism is transformed into hope. God's people never stopped asking for a king. But they learned to stop asking for one like the "other nations" had. Now they asked for one like God himself.

As God's people in the 21st century after the advent of that Heavenly King, we face a challenge that is no less acute. As our nations grow more desperate for justice, can we hold on to the hope that the one who began his reign will bring it to completion?

LORD Jesus, come! Bring us your justice and the abundance of your reign!

Prabo & Dorothy Mihindukulasuriya
Colombo, Sri Lanka
Seminary Lecturer and Teacher
Regent Alums (MCS, 2000 & MCS, 2006)

15

Romans 15:1-13

In an Entirely Different Place

*E*ndurance and encouragement. I recognise my need for both instantly; a dozen scenarios pop quickly to mind where these two ingredients have been in short supply. In an equal instant, I assume endurance to be my job—head down, jaw clamped, a lone runner on a long highway, doggedly swinging the next foot forward. And I fear encouragement that is too facile; the quick slap on the back as I trudge along that highway.

But Romans 15 reminds me that endurance is not solitary, and encouragement is not cheap. Moreover, Paul assures me that both are gifts from God. That fact takes me off the lonely highway and puts me in an entirely different place, one of community and shared endurance, a place where encouragement sinks deeply into a well of genuine hope.

But Paul has a trio of preoccupations here, and the third is unity. He has a different tone entirely on that issue, one best described as pleading. The epitome of strength, one assumes Paul was not a man often given to pleading, but here he is, practically on his knees begging his listeners to get along. He naturally asks God to help his readers with unity, as he does with endurance and encouragement. Yet with each, God can only do so much. Hence, the pleading tone: Paul knows it is we who must endure, we who must offer and receive encouragement, and we who must bear with one another. Or not. The choice is ours.

And what of Advent? What of preparation for God? We will need plenty of each as we make our way to Bethlehem, and ultimately to the way of the risen Christ: endurance, encouragement and unity.

Patti Towler
Vice President, External Relations and Legal Counsel,
Regent College
Regent Alum (DipCS, 1996)

Isaiah 9:2-7

Longing for Peace

eace is a desired but elusive concept. We long for peace in our hearts and in our world. However, it often seems unattainable. It is antithetical to our busy lifestyles, not to mention our geo-political reality. Countless books are written about how to achieve peace in one's personal life, family life, or state of mind. There are books that examine the lack of peace in our world, and others that strategize how the world can have peace. There are various organizations that aim for peace, in the environment, in the Middle East, and in our neighbourhoods. Well-meaning ideas circulate regarding peace; if only human beings could be more selfless, more tolerant, more just, then peace would be attainable. These are all noble and worthy objectives, and they show us the extent to which people yearn for peace. This passage, however, reminds us that peace, or more precisely, *shalom*—wholeness—is act of God.

According to Isaiah, King Ahaz's lack of trust in *Yahweh* compromised his kingdom and further led the Israelites astray into commotion and chaos. Isaiah prophesies God's promise of a future King that will bring *shalom*; this King will be called "Prince of Peace." Israel is called to trust in this future hope of *shalom*. This King is the promise of light in darkness, of joy and celebration, of restoration and endless peace.

In today's seemingly dark and unsettling world we too are called to trust. For a child has been born to us, he has come! We trust in Christ's leadership in our lives, knowing that God has made peace a present day reality by giving us his Son, and that God continues to work out peace in our lives and in our world. He will work it out into fulfilment.

Sarah Shih
Hampstead, QC
Writer and Mother
Regent Alum (MCS, 2005)

Matthew 3:1-12

Repentance

"Prepare the way of the Lord, make his paths straight." We see from Matthew's Gospel that John's prophetic work included not just a baptism of repentance, but also a fiery "preaching ministry," predicting the coming of an individual more powerful and more worthy than he is. This one who is to come will cut down those trees that do not bear "good fruit," separating the wheat from the chaff.

What are we to make of this text, one with fiery, unsettling and judgmental rhetoric? Isn't Advent a time of love and caring, a time when we are more disposed to the warmth of the burning Yule log than the heat of the fire of judgment?

I think Advent is a time for those things—for love, caring and warmth in the midst of our preparation for the advent of our Lord Jesus. But our reading reminds us that our preparation is also more than that. The preparation of Advent should also cause us to be uncomfortable, to contemplate those dark corners in our lives, those places that require our repentance to prepare the way for Jesus to be born again in our midst. True preparation, truly "getting ready" for Christmas is not about "making a list and checking it twice," nor is it about the busyness of shopping, travelling and entertaining. Instead, John's words remind us that true Advent preparation, truly "getting ready for Christmas" means truly being self-reflective, exploring our hearts for those places in need of God's grace and forgiveness.

John's words also remind us that no one is immune from the scrutiny of the "coming one." But the good news is that all of us are invited to prepare for the coming Messiah through repentance and committing our lives in faith to Christ anew.

Bob Derrenbacker
Assistant Professor of New Testament Studies,
Regent College

Isaiah 11:1-10

His Words

*I*n contrast to the Assyrians, the coming Messiah is an unlikely warrior. Not only is he a shoot from a tree-stump, but also his person and weapons are rather un-warrior-like. He is endowed with the gifts of a governor and a spiritual leader as well as those of an army chief; and when it comes to his duties as judge, his concern is for the poor and needy rather than the rich and mighty. The unlikely end-result of his reign is a "peace that passes all understanding." He achieves his peace with very unlikely weapons: "the rod of his mouth" and "the breath of his lips."

The Messiah's ways of battling—words, communication—make him very vulnerable. Words, our initiative at relationship, can be rejected, misunderstood, ridiculed. By communicating, one bestows on the other(s) the responsibility to respond. The ultimate Word of God resounded when the shoot of Jesse was born on this earth. As foretold by the prophet, Jesus lived and acted as the unlikely warrior: his words—and his silences—were his weapons.

We cannot hear his words with our ears today, so it is easier to ignore the call to respond. It is easier to shut the book and forget about the words, or analyze their meaning without truly responding.

But the child we are expecting this Advent still uses the breath of his lips and the rod of his mouth to achieve his victory. His Spirit brings the written word alive, and he speaks through those around us: through their words of comfort and their cries for help. Today, may we be able to respond, and may our words, too, be a means of establishing his peace.

Dora Bernhardt
Budapest, Hungary
Associate Lecturer, Karoli University of the Hungarian Reformed Church
Regent Alum (ThM, 2003)

Isaiah 25:1-9

His Love is Not Shiny

Too often, I find myself trying to direct my life. I muscle my way into the "shoulds" and "have-tos" of the world. I construct my identity based on the glamour of a modern city or lives of famous people, but end up lost and trampled in the makeshift ways of the world. Like Israel, I compare myself to those around me and see how small and vulnerable I am. The world can be harsh and I can become discouraged and beaten down. The powerful crush the weak and the strong-willed crush their own souls with the unquenchable thirst for youth, influence and security.

But as the prophet Isaiah calls a ragged and downtrodden people to remember to whom they belong, we are reminded that God is sovereign. He tears down whole cities and their powerful leaders. He has planned and directed everything long before we were born. And his sovereignty is shown by his love. He spreads a beautiful feast for the poor in spirit, relationally broken, and those thirsty for love. His love is not shiny like a Christmas present under the tree, but it is the biggest gift we can receive. God is our God, who rules this world, bears our pain, and loves us unconditionally. It is his love that nourishes our souls; and, beyond the grasp of fear and grief, brings a true peace.

Rest in knowing that God is in control of all that has happened, and all that will happen. And in this Advent season, rest in knowing that he has given the best gift—peace that is beyond our fear and grief, with the birth of his Son, Jesus Christ.

Alice Christie Chen
Continuing Studies Coordinator,
Regent College
Regent Alum (MDiv, 2001)

Isaiah 40:1-11

Look!

"*C*ry out!" a voice is told.

"Look! Here is your God," the voice tells us.

Can you see him? What do you see? Comfort for a weary people. Peace for a divided kingdom.

Do you see the glorious celebration as the warrior King returns to his beloved city? The city suddenly comes alive with pageantry. Women come running. These women, who every day imagined themselves to be widows, come running to see if their men are with the King. Oh, the King! Children who long to see their daddies come running, hoping to catch a glimpse. Is my daddy with the King? Oh, the King!

The King comes into the great plaza of the city, bringing with him his reward, the spoils of the battle. Women and men, boys and girls all push in to see the treasure, the reward. What has the warrior King brought back? What could it be?!

What do you see?

This mighty Warrior, the sovereign LORD, brings salvation. He brings deliverance. Can you see it? Look! Coming in behind the King, into the center of his beloved city, a throng of his redeemed people is brought back from exile. Streams and streams of weary prisoners freed from slavery return to that glorious city! And if you look closely, there you are. There I am. He chose to fight for us. To die for us. To bring us back for all to see.

But that's not all. That mighty arm which redeems is an arm tender enough to carry the lambs. This warrior King is also a tender Shepherd. He tends and gathers, he carries and leads. Comfort, comfort my people. The peace has been hard won. The warrior Shepherd redeems. His reward is with him. We are there.

Paul Voltmer
Salzburg, Austria
Director, befreit leben
Regent Alum (MDiv, 2002)

Isaiah 42:1-9

The True Image of God

In the darkness, people clung to their idols. They looked on the LORD with terror and worshipped wood and gold. Hoping for security, they anchored these idols down with nails. But their worship of these empty things did not give them the protection they yearned for; their idols could not administer true justice or peace. The people stumbled in the dark, worshipping what their own hands had made.

God, however, did not leave them in that darkness. With all the incorrigible joy of a lover, he presented them with his best gift: his Servant. Idols are always tyrants in the end; the Servant would bring a powerful justice that would not crush, but defend the weak. He would not simply provide, but be a light: opening eyes, freeing captives, and bringing about true peace. Only he would be worthy of their worship, the true Image of God.

When I think of this joyous call to look to the Servant, I am reminded of God's compassion. People clung to empty idols they could touch, so God gave them his Son: tangible, personal, and streaming with life. Those in Isaiah's day had only the promise of such a Servant, but we live in his reality. The Light has come, and ultimately he will conquer any darkness.

We may still live with pain and injustice, blindness and bondage; we may still rely on what we have made with our own hands. Advent reminds us, though, that the Servant of the LORD has come. He brings about true justice and reconciling peace through his Spirit and his people. He offers us freedom.

Kirsten Behee
Artist and Campus Pastor,
Simon Fraser University
Regent Alum (MCS Arts, 2007)

Isaiah 49:1-13

Hidden in the Purposes of God

The Chosen Servant is an arrow prepared for flight – tipped with sharpened bronze, shaft shined, feathers trimmed and aligned. Then the Servant is placed in the quiver, a dark and hidden place, ready for the moment when the Great Warrior's hand will seize him and place him on the bow.

The quiver brings to mind the many hidden years of Jesus' life. His childhood, of which we know only that "the child grew and became strong; he was filled with wisdom, and the grace of God was upon him." (Lk. 2: 40). His adolescence, of which we know only his precocious awareness of his "Father's business" as he debates with the teachers in the Jerusalem temple, and then that "he went down to Nazareth with [Mary and Joseph] and was obedient to them" (Lk. 2: 51). The adult years until he is thirty, during which even members of his own family seem to have become restive at his slowness to demonstrate his supernatural knowledge and power in a public way.

Hidden in the quiver. Waiting God's time. Called, prepared and now concealed. The Servant feels forgotten...or a failure. He cries out: "I have laboured to no purpose; I have spent my strength in vain and for nothing."

Suddenly, a second voice speaks, and his monologue becomes a dialogue with the Sovereign LORD himself: "It is too small a thing for you...to restore the tribes of Jacob...I will also make you a light for the Gentiles,...[to] bring my salvation to the ends of the earth."

The arrow hidden in the quiver will one day be strung on the bow of the cross, and the Mighty Archer will bring in a covenant that extends to all of the earth's people.

Maxine Hancock
Professor of Interdisciplinary Studies & Spiritual Theology,
Regent College

Isaiah 50:4-11

Everlasting Dawn

*F*or the Servant and his fellow Israelites, the night is long. This night is one of suffering under the foot of an oppressor. In exile for their idolatry, Israel grows restless. The Servant of the LORD tells them to wait for their redemption…and suffer. The Servant closes his eyes and his ears are opened. In the beginning, the voice of the LORD spoke into the darkness. Shrouded in darkness, the Servant listens for the voice that called forth the dawn. Morning by morning, the Servant hears this voice and speaks, "Let those who walk in darkness, who have no light, trust in the name of the LORD and rely on his God."

But Israel will not wait in darkness. In arrogance, Israel sets out to hasten the redemption that the LORD has promised. Fires are kindled, plans are made and torches are lit. With torches, the world seeks to push back the darkness and find a way forward. With fire, the world declares war on the terrors of the night.

Yet, for rebellious Israel, the only way into Canaan was through the wilderness (Num. 14:44-45). For idolatrous Israel, the only way home is through suffering. When God clothes the heavens in darkness, igniting fires is an act of rebellion and torch-lit paths will only lead astray; their end is destruction. As always, the way forward is to stay near the LORD and he is near his Servant in exile.

While we await the final and everlasting dawn, when night shall be no more, let us ask for open ears that we may hear the voice of the LORD and endure the darkness.

Ian W. Panth
Assistant Manager, Regent Bookstore
Regent Alum (MCS, 2001)

Isaiah 52:1-12

Rise Up!

*O*ne summer I walked along a side street in Cairo, Egypt. Down to my left, on the sidewalk and against a building, I glanced at a pile of dusty rags, rags that suddenly moved, just a bit. To my amazement, the rags formed themselves into a human being. Reading Isaiah reminded me of my surprise that day.

"Shake yourself from the dust, rise up...!" God calls to his people. At the end of Isaiah 51, there is a vivid picture of what it had been like for Jerusalem to drink from the "cup of staggering" and the bowl of God's wrath: her tormentors commanded her to bow down, so that they could walk on her. And she'd done it: she'd made her back like the ground or the street.

"Shake yourself from the dust, rise up...!" It's our call in Advent, too: the call to recognise and acknowledge our dusty state – both as we were originally created from the earth, and as we were pronounced "dust" after the sin of Adam and Eve. But it's our call to wake up as well, to spring up and shake off the dust, to know the LORD's name – he says, "Here I am." It's our call to know him intimately through the One he sends, and to be pure, to be re-created by this One who brings good news, *shalom*, salvation.

Funny, as we wend our way towards winter (summer in the Southern Hemisphere), we read Isaiah 52 and sense spring in the call to wake up. During these Advent days, listen for the joyful singing of the sentinels and look for the LORD's return. With him before us and behind, we'll see the salvation of our God. Awake, and clothe yourselves in garments of splendour!

Libbie Weber
Albuquerque, NM
Episcopal Priest, Diocese of Rio Grande
Regent Alum (MCS, 1998)

Isaiah 52:13-53:12

Love Born

*W*e're more used to thinking about this "suffering servant" passage at Easter. But any reflection on the birth of Jesus that leaves out his death and resurrection is missing the central truth about Christmas. Our usual reasoning goes like this: Why was Jesus born? Because he had to die. Why did he have to die? Because of our sins. Why did our sins require his death? Because God's justice requires that sin be punished. But why Jesus and not us? Because Jesus was sinless, and thus the only one who could bear God's wrath in our place. Jesus was a sacrifice that God's justice required. So when we come to Isaiah 53 we read, "the LORD has laid on him the iniquity of us all" (6), and "it was the LORD's will to cause him to suffer" (10) as though the main thing being revealed here is God's wrath.

But there is another way to read of God's suffering Servant in Isaiah 53: that it is not God's wrath which is shown on the cross, but God's love, the love which (in Luke's parable), without any sacrifice went running towards the returning son; the love which (as many Christmas carols reflect), was born as a baby. This reading takes its clue from verse 4: "Surely he took up our pain and bore our suffering, yet we considered him punished by God, stricken by him, and afflicted." Clearly it's a mistake to see him as the object of God's wrath. He suffers rather from our wrath (a wrath shown soon enough by the visit of Herod's soldiers to Bethlehem). Why was Jesus born? Because only by becoming a helpless human whom we "despised and rejected" could God show us the love that lies at the heart of his creation.

Loren E. Wilkinson
Professor of Interdisciplinary Studies and Philosophy,
Regent College

Isaiah 60:1-3

Fresh Wind

*T*here is no Yuletide sentimentality in Advent. Peace will not come by wishing for it. Peace will not come by imagining it. Peace will not come by God waving a magic wand.

No, peace will come by God wielding a sceptre and a sword. Peace will come only in the drastic rearranging of the deranged, and if that sounds violent, it is. Today's passage follows a prophetic promise of doom in chapter 59 that God's justice will arrive like a hurricane.

So today's promise of light, the almost-unbelievable promise that we ourselves can shine as we reflect the brilliance of the shaft streaming down on us from God's kindly face, is breathtaking. Indeed, it is breath-giving as life and light come to the dying and dark.

We cannot possibly disperse the choking murk of the accumulated smog of millennia of sin—our own and others'. We cannot venture a single step in confidence, given our moral blindness and a world system we simply cannot trust for justice.

But God can blow the miasma away and leave only fresh air. God can roll back the clouds and let the sunshine in. And he will do so upon his own people for the benefit of all people.

God has shone his light in our hearts, the apostle affirms (2 Cor. 4:6), "to give the light of the knowledge of the glory of God in the face of Jesus Christ." The *shekinah* is here, now, in each of us filled with the very Spirit of God.

Let us look around, then, at the gloom in which our world is submerged. Let us reflect on the stifling darkness that once stuffed our hearts and still takes up too much space. And let us petition the Wind/Breath/Spirit of God to blow through us all again.

John G. Stackhouse, Jr.
Sangwoo Youtong Chee Professor of Theology and Culture,
Regent College

Isaiah 61

A Glimpse of His Riches

I wasn't raised to serve—or really, to even think about the poor. We had a fulltime housekeeper, a gardener, someone to drive us to ballet lessons. So when God called me to vocational ministry during my studies at Regent College, I assumed I would be working among the upper middleclass. An Anglican minister, no doubt. With a country club membership. After all, great ministry could be done on the tennis courts, n'est-ce pas?

A winter's night found us off campus, listening to a lecture about a very unique church-plant started by Paddy Ducklow. Using ingenuity, wit and sheer determination, Ducklow had transformed meagre resources into manna. Much manna. And now, just a few years later, he was feeding, clothing and educating hundreds, every single month.

Simple, yet life-changing. Disturbingly easy. And yet…amazingly, shockingly, sinfully rare.

Before the class ended, I was weeping uncontrollably. I could not speak. I could not drive home. Why weren't other churches doing this? Why wasn't everyone? Why wasn't I?

Could any of us ever claim innocence again?

Three years later, as I stood among the ruins of Atlanta's inner city, doling out chicken to the hungry and praying for the sick, I remembered that cold Vancouver night when God broke my heart. With the grace that only a Heavenly Father could offer, he escorted me to the door of his kingdom and offered a glimpse of his greatest riches. Not mansions, Mercedes or Manolo Blahniks. Not even stained glass windows or candelabras. Just the hungry, the lonely, the destitute.

And, the brokenhearted.

Annabelle Robertson
Santa Barbara County, CA
Journalist and Author
Regent Alum (MDiv, 1997)

Psalm 146

Sing With Us

*L*et us consider the Psalms as a prayer book and hymnal of the Jewish characters we encounter in Scripture surrounding Jesus' birth. Hear these words from Psalm 146 being sung by Elizabeth while her miracle baby is sleeping: "Praise the LORD, my soul. / I will praise the LORD all my life; / I will sing praise to my God as long as I live."

We often hear that the Jews were longing for a political leader to free them from Rome. I wonder if they questioned that longing when they sang this Psalm. Listen to Zechariah, unable to speak, mouthing these words in the temple: "Do not put your trust in princes, / in human beings: who cannot save."

Picture Joseph finding reassurance as he sings, "Blessed are those whose help is the God of Jacob, / whose hope is in the LORD their God. / He is the Maker of heaven and earth, / the sea, and everything in them— / he remains faithful forever."

And, now, hear Mary, not on the day she sang similar words in her Magnificat, but later, on a day when she is visibly pregnant, perhaps a little frightened, and likely misunderstood in the community. Did she find comfort in these words? "He upholds the cause of the oppressed / and gives food to the hungry. / The LORD sets prisoners free, / the LORD gives sight to the blind, / the LORD lifts up those who are bowed down, / the LORD loves the righteous."

As we begin this day, aware of the many upheavals and injustices in the world, and with our own hopes for human solutions, are we willing to trust in the God who reigns on high and yet comes and dwells in our midst? Are we willing to listen—to sing?

Andrea Tisher
Music & Worship Coordinator
Regent College
Regent Alum (DipCS, 2006; MCS Candidate)

Romans 13:11-14

Know the Time, Recognise the Hour!

*N*otably, Saint Augustine's life was turned around at the reading of this text, as it so starkly contrasts night-life with light-life – the Christian's charge to put away the "works of darkness" and to put on the "weaponry of light," the LORD Jesus Christ himself. What a strange but startling thought, to "get dressed" in Jesus! How did the apostle arrive at this thought? The answer is recognising the *kairos*—the advent of an appointed moment. Let me illustrate.

Sleeping in the bush, here under the African night-sky, gave us countless waking hours in the company of carnivorous clamour. It made us peculiarly attentive to that signal moment when the heavens publicize that dawn is declaring day, and night is a fugitive. In South African history, this moment was demonstrated when the name *kairos* was chosen for a document presented to the Apartheid Government shortly before its demise. This *kairos* pronounced—and demanded —a transformation into light for the imminent new epoch.

By saying, therefore, that we must "know the *kairos*," Paul is alerting his hearers to the fact that the day of final salvation is dawning. A new age has burst upon our world through the resurrection of Christ. Redemptive infancy that lay quietly in the Christmas cradle will soon be unveiled in maturity with trumpet-and-shout as the once crucified One returns in glory (compare 1 Thess. 4:16-18; Tit. 2:11-14). Even as we rest this night, we remain awakened to the at-hand-ness of that day. We hasten ourselves to be clothed in Christ!

We are "sons of light and sons of day"; we "belong to the day" (1 Thess. 5:5, 8)!

James B. Krohn
Cape Town, South Africa
Associate Professor of Theology,
George Whitefield College
Regent Alum (MCS, 1997)

Isaiah 35:1-10

Dear Pilgrim, Take Hope

I don't know if my pecan trees are old and tired or young and tired. I live in a neighbourhood where pecan trees rise eighty to a hundred feet high into the burning Texas sky, towering reddish-brown canopies, and bearers of a buttery fruit. But this year they've turned strange. All summer long they've been falling apart, losing limbs, with a kind of wild fever. Thick, scaly branches rip away, crack the air with an unnerving screeching sound, and then plummet with a whoosh and whirl of leaves and a ka-whoomp into the ground. All down my block, day and night, branches crash on top of cars and roofs and lawns, yielding up a great whine of chainsaws.

Good things that should be strong and unchanging are falling apart: trees, marriages, Olympic athletes, childhood dreams, homes in New Orleans, old books, friendships, a beautiful pair of shoes, the human heart. Seeing so much brokenness makes us sad and even despair.

But the words of Isaiah interrupt our downward spiral. Hang in there, dear pilgrim. Brokenness will not have the last word. The LORD speaks: "Strengthen weakened hands, / make firm feeble knees; / Say to those who are fearful-hearted: / 'Be strong! Do not fear!'"

Blind, deaf, lame, and dumb—of body and heart—will be made whole. Wastelands will blossom. The hot sands will become a cool oasis. Wrongs will be made right. And the redeemed of our beautiful King will come dancing home with halos of everlasting joy.

There is a tiredness in the earth, I suppose, that has nothing to do with age. It is a tiredness of living in a world where things break down, fall apart. Yet the prophet calls out to us. Dear pilgrim, take hope.

Gladness and joy shall overtake thee
Sorrows and sighing shall flee away!

W. David O. Taylor
Austin, TX
Arts Pastor,
Regent Alum (ThM, 2000)

31

Matthew 11:2-11

Signs

*J*ohn. At the Jordan: Confident. Bold. Insulting. Offensive in message and manner, tongue and tunic. Chastising the only king of the Jews most people knew: "Adulterer!" Rebuking the only religious teachers most ever heard: "Vipers!" Miraculous conception. Cousin of Jesus. The Elijah to come. Christbaptizer. Witness to the Spirit-dove and the Fatherly commendation: "This is the one to come!"

John. In prison: "Are you the one to come? The one I predicted?"

John, is that you? Are those doubts real?

And why not? Did Jesus meet anyone's expectations for the Messiah? The Pharisees'? The Essenes'? The Zealots'? The Apostles'? Perhaps not even John's? Anyone's? Well, perhaps Isaiah's. But even Isaiah would have been surprised at who came and how he came, but not, I think, at what he did. For Isaiah had said, "Look here to know the One who is coming!" Look here for signs of the Messiah: eyes opened, ears unstopped. Physically. Spiritually. Arid places and arid souls irrigated with water that lives. Disabled feet and disabled souls gifted with ability and a reason to dance. For once, news from a King the poor could welcome. Yet it was all this that moved John from the greatest to the least. The greatest of those who looked forward; and, of those who looked back, the least.

And these signs of Isaiah's, what became of them? Did John accept their testimony? And these signs, is this not what the Messiah continues to do? Heal, gift, restore, resurrect. Resist and reverse the anti-creation, anti-relational effects of sin. Yes—better go tell John!

Thus while promise opened our day, it ends with fulfillment. Of what? Love. The Creator's, the Messiah's, the King's. For John. For me. For you.

Brian Williams
Topeka, KS
Teacher of Philosophy and Theology,
Cair Paravel Latin School
Regent Alum (MCS, 2000)

Psalm 96

All Nations Will Sing

*T*his great Hebrew hymn looks back to the triumphal return of the ark of God to Jerusalem (1 Chron. 16) even while celebrating Israel's deliverance from Babylonian captivity and the restoration of the new temple in Jerusalem. The real thrust of the psalm is, however, towards the coming reign of the Messiah, Jesus Christ. Its messianic vision weaves together a beautiful tapestry of three themes—Celebration, Submission and Hope—in an expression of true worship in which exaltation of the incomparable *Yahweh* flows inevitably into a passionate call to declare his glory among the nations.

A recent visit with simple, first-generation believers in a remote village in North India helped this psalm come alive for me as never before. Genuine devotion and spontaneous gratitude expressed in joyful singing and graceful dance; the roll of native drums, brilliant splashes of colour in tribal costume and floral tributes blended in a moving invocation to worship. This was not just shallow revelry. Their lilting chants explained why they bowed with deep reverence to King Jesus, and readily gave up their former ways in submission to his teaching. For centuries they had been outcastes within the social structure of the dominant religion, excluded from high-caste privileges of access to education, land and civic rights. The most brutal reality of their dark existence: no access to God and no hope for the future…

…Until they heard the good news that the God of all the earth has come and established his reign on earth. That he will rule with truth and justice and has come to set everything right. That the LORD of all creation loves all people equally but has a special place in his heart for the poor, the marginalized, the outcast.

Ivan Satyavrata
Kolkata, India
Senior Pastor, Calcutta Assembly of God
Regent Alum (MCS, 1991)

Hebrews 1:1-4

The final Word

*M*any think that this theologically loaded text is the core of an early Christian hymn. And what a song it sings! In the events beginning in Bethlehem, the Living and invisible God has finally and fully spoken to us. And God's speech turns out to be the Christmas Child! "In these last days God has spoken to us in Son." Not "a Son," or even, "the Son." Just Son. Jesus. Mary's son, God's Son.

Why is Jesus and no other the final word? The text sings seven reasons. He is the "heir of all things." Everything and everyone is stamped with, "belongs to Jesus." He is the Creator of all things, "through whom he made the world." He is heir because the Maker owns all he makes. He is "the radiance of God's glory," the shining forth of what makes God be God. He is "the exact representation of God's nature." You want to know who God is and what God is like? You look at Jesus. He "upholds all things by the word of his power." "He's got the whole world in his hands" is more than folksy poetry: it is literally true. Meaning, therefore, that we can lay down the horrible burden of trying to keep everything together ourselves. He "made purification for our sins." Literally it is, "He himself." No one else did because no one else could. He has done everything that needs to be done about sin! Sing it from the mountaintops! Then, he "sat down at the right hand." The One born in Bethlehem lived, died, was raised from the dead, and is lifted up to the throne of the universe where he lives as LORD and Intercessor and Lover of God's people.

O Spirit of the Living God, through this text sing us into the joy of Christmas!

Darrell W. Johnson
Associate Professor of Pastoral Theology,
Regent College

Titus 2:11-14

The Appearing

To read Titus 2:1-10 in isolation is to confront a long list of behaviours, some of which should be practised and others avoided, and to sense that the Christian life is epitomised in conduct and performance. But to embrace the next four verses is to ground ethical practices in Christian doctrine and to recognise that while human action should be honourable, it is at its best when it is rooted in the "appearance of the grace of God."

Significantly, Paul concludes his instructions with the reminder that the "appearance of the grace of God," as personified in the birth, life, death and resurrection of Jesus, is the foundation for all human performance. The grace of God is not only redemptive in that it brings our salvation, it is also instructive and educative as it makes us aware of which actions and attitudes should be refused with a resounding "no" and which should be practised with an unbridled "yes." This life is to be lived not only with a look back at the original appearance but also a look ahead to the next appearance, an act that has God's ultimate pleasure in mind—finally he will have a people for himself.

Ironically, the frenzy of our contemporary lives seems to intensify at Christmas. We find ourselves on a treadmill, grasping for the off switch, fighting for air. The appearance of the grace of God does not create inactivity or passivity, but provides grounding for our behaviour to be shaped by more sustainable motives. Our lives become less hurried and more peaceful when they are rooted in love and grace. It is good to meditate on Christ's appearance and its gentle implications. I pray that, as we move through this day, we will remember that God's kingdom is not totally dependent on our engagement.

Rod J. K. Wilson
President, Professor of Counselling and Psychology,
Regent College

Titus 3:4-7

Love Breaks In

*A*dvent whispers a promise that Love is coming. For those walking through a season of darkness and suffering, there often emerges a longing for more than the mere hope that one's personal circumstances will change. The Holy Spirit whispers that what we deeply long for is a Love that will break into our seemingly futile existence, pursue us, and when it finds us, change us so completely that we can experience rest in the midst of any kind of turmoil.

In Titus 3:4-7 Paul reminds the Cretan Christians that the Triune God broke into their sordid, messy lives through the most intimate and profound means possible. He came in spirit (Holy Spirit) and flesh (Jesus Christ) to shake up their disobedient existence and awaken their hearts to know his own. Paul recounts how the drama unfolded. In a lavish act of mercy flowing from his love and kindness, God broke into humanity's shadowy existence and made himself known. Then the Holy Spirit began the process of spiritually washing each soul—preparing it to receive God's salvific love. Finally, through Christ's willingness to be limited to human form and to suffer and die for others, each soul was offered the opportunity to receive unearned and unexpected deliverance from its sinful state, with the assurance of a love that was free and priceless.

The Triune God is still unfolding this drama of love in our lives today. God breaks in, and the Holy Spirit bathes us in love; thus he rebirths in us a capacity to receive transforming love that cleanses and remakes us. Then Christ comes to remind us that this Love will sustain us in the midst of suffering, and with it he brings the promise that deliverance has come, is coming, will come.

Jodi Heatly
Austin, TX
Writer, Hospice Nurse
Regent Alum (MCS, 2003)

Matthew 2:1-12

Mysterious Grace

he activity of the magi frames this narrative (2:1-2, 9-12). It is a narrative pervaded by the language of kingship: the magi come seeking a king and, encountering conflicting claims on their loyalty, they find that they must choose, as must we all. They choose wisely, worshipping the Christ and turning away from Herod—guided by the same mysterious grace that has led them to truth by way of a flawed divinatory method. Their experience is reminiscent of Balaam's story (Num. 22-24): he, too, comes from the east, practising magic and divination; he discerns a king and a star in Israel; he serves a manipulative pagan king, whose intentions are frustrated by God. In the end, though, he aligns himself with that king and suffers the consequences (Num. 31:8,16); the magi, by God's mercy, heed his warning and so are honoured among the outsiders and foreigners who have recognised him in every age.

The activity of Herod intrudes upon that of the magi (2:3-8). It obstructs while seeming to further their quest, for Herod also finds that he must choose between two kings. He chooses foolishly, promising worship of the Christ but clinging to his own autonomy—even though he is guided by the overt grace of orthodox religion, whose wisdom he later twists to devilish ends. Thus he implicitly forfeits the kingship to which he clings; and in Matthew, his name is divorced from the title of king after this encounter with the truth of Christ's advent.

Even at his birth, in a scene where he is seemingly inactive, Jesus exposes the complex responses of many hearts: joy, and consternation; true worship, and feigned; the giving of gifts, and the taking of life.

So may he search, and purify, our hearts.

David Clemens
Associate Professor, Biblical Languages
Regent College

Matthew 2:13-23

The Beginning

I find this passage difficult to read. The story of Mary and Joseph's narrow escape with their new son and Herod's massacre of the infants is jarring, even terrifying. Why is it here? Why does Matthew interrupt the warmth of Jesus' birth-story with this image of horror, and imply that Herod's gruesome act was a fulfilment of prophecy?

We wrestle here, perhaps, with the meaning of the word "fulfill." Was Rachel's weeping (Jer. 31:16) a prediction, which was brought to fruition at this abhorrent moment in history when the women of Israel wept? I don't think this is Matthew's intention. Instead, he uses Jeremiah 31 to make two points: the advent of this baby is a threat to earthly kingdoms; the advent of this baby is hope for God's people.

Although Herod's rebellion against Christ's rule caused immense grief among God's people, the prophecy of Jeremiah 31 is not about weeping. It is about the end of weeping. It speaks of the love of God and the establishment of his kingdom. The passage states with bold hope: yes, there is weeping now—but one day it will end. It proclaims Jesus' birth as the beginning of that end.

Matthew's use of Jeremiah 31 does not lift the weight of present suffering— the world still struggles against Jesus' reign, and this struggle causes pain—but it invites us into a hope that grows gradually stronger. Sometime before you sleep tonight, read Jeremiah 31 in its entirety. Hear, especially, the call of Jeremiah 31:3, "I have loved you with an everlasting love; I have drawn you with unfailing kindness." Hear it in the context of a mother's weeping for her children. Until we celebrate the next advent of Christ we continue to weep, for ourselves and for a world in rebellion, but we do so knowing that the end has already begun.

Stacey Gleddiesmith
Development Writer,
Regent College
Regent Alum (MDiv, 2007)

Luke 1:5-25

Sweet, Perfect Time

here was a time when they had asked why. That is, at the times when they weren't asking for a child. They had both lived righteous lives. They had taken their faith seriously. But there had been no offspring. They had stopped asking. It was late in the day. God wasn't going to show up. Once in awhile there were the whispers. Perhaps Elizabeth and Zechariah were harbouring secret sins. That was why her womb was cursed. They weren't sure which was worst. The absence of a child. Or the whispering. Or the not knowing why.

But life had some consolations. At least Zechariah had the opportunity to offer incense in the Holy Place. Here was a privilege that happened only once in a priest's lifetime, if it happened at all. It was his moment. Elizabeth was proud, and she made sure her man had on his best robes.

And when they least expect it, God shows up. The angel Gabriel is sent with the good news. God had heard their prayers. God had heard their prayers all along. And God was answering. Not only would they have a child, their child would be the forerunner of the Messiah! This is just like God, taking his own sweet and perfect time to answer us, giving us much more than we asked for, and blessing us when we least expect it.

LORD, *as we observe another Advent, remind us that you have not forsaken us and that you have heard our prayers. Remind us, O* LORD, *that in the fullness of time you will answer and that we can stake our lives on your faithfulness. Remind us, O* LORD, *of the joy that awaits us so that we can start rejoicing even now.*

Soo-Inn Tan
Singapore
Director, Graceworks
Regent Alum (ThM, 1986)

39

Luke 1:26-38

God's Yes

hy does it matter where Jesus sits? Conceiving and bearing and naming —all the familiar elements of birth are present in this text, yet so is the matter of a throne.

The setting is Nazareth of Galilee, an off-the-beaten-path kind of place. In this place, to a girl who is young in a world that values age, female in a world ruled by men, and poor on top of it all, Gabriel, the mighty angel-messenger, descends. "You will become pregnant," says Gabriel, "and give birth to a son...and the LORD God will give him the throne of his ancestor David."

The words hail from an earlier story, the theological centre of the entire Samuel writings. God proclaims that David will not build God a house, but God will build David a house. This is the central promise to David: a dynasty, a kingdom and a forever-throne, set within the promise that someday the world would be made right.

Hundreds of years later, Gabriel brings the best of all news—in Jesus, this is the time. Why does it matter where Jesus sits? It matters because this is God keeping his promise. God said he would establish David's throne forever and in Jesus, this is what God is doing. Jesus is God's "Yes."

The invitation of Advent is to learn, along with Mary, to say "Yes" to God's "Yes" in Jesus. Yes to every small thing that Jesus asks us. Yes to love and joy and peace. Yes to acts of generosity and justice and selflessness. Yes to self-examination and to repentance and to change. May the prayer that is being formed in us this Advent be our response to our promise-keeping God—Yes, for all that will be, yes.

Barbara Mutch
Vice President Academic,
Carey Theological College

Luke 1:39-56

Ponder Anew

*T*he Magnificat is reenacted in one scene of the riveting theatrical production, "The Christmas Story," produced by the Church of the Holy Trinity in downtown Toronto. The production, which has run for some sixty years, is enjoyed by many city dwellers each advent season. What makes this particular performance so memorable is that "The Story" is reenacted without words, except for a narrator bathed in a single spotlight reading a harmonized version of the Gospel infancy narratives and a trained choir singing from the balcony at the back of the church. The actors, dressed in traditional garb, use only hand and body motions to express the Gospel message.

One of the most dramatic scenes is when a dazzling angel rises from the depths of the stage amidst dissipating mist. The angel addresses Mary, informing her that she will bear the Christ-child. And somehow, through hand gestures and facial expressions, the wordless Mary conveys her initial fear, followed by a sense of humility and gratitude for this unexpected gift from God. Mary's obedient spirit and pure heart shine as clear as the Nativity Star that the three wise men follow. The Magnificat is Mary's compelling hymn of praise to God for the good things he has done. The hymn captures in small measure the deep outpouring of Mary's heart as she responds to the news that she will bear the Messiah.

May we, like Mary, ponder anew the good gifts that God has graciously showered upon us, especially our LORD Jesus Christ. And may we respond with thanks, praise and a song in our hearts as we respond to the call we have received to bear Christ's life in our world. Amen.

Cindy Derrenbacker
Director,
The John Richard Allison Library
Regent College

Luke 1:57-80

The Real Disturbance Begins

*A*mid much rejoicing—made all the more poignant for being under Roman domination—they come on the eighth day to circumcise the child, ratifying Israel's special relationship to the one true God. If one cannot control international politics, then the smaller domains take on greater significance. The real disturbance begins in this little village. Naming, after all, is how we make sense of our world. In uncertain times, family becomes more important and the boy needs to know his lineage.

Something even larger than family is afoot and, tellingly, the first break begins not with Rome but family tradition. This child is not about the family, but the nation. In reversing the ancient exilic judgment his name is to be Johanan because now, recalling Israel's true lineage, "*Yahweh* has shown favour," unbelieving Zechariah, in not living up to his name "*Yahweh* remembers," had earlier been struck dumb. Perhaps, like Israel itself, if he would not faithfully confess his own identity, then he would not speak at all. So that when he now, in faith, asserts the promise, "His name is John," he speaks the very words of God. Under the awesome and holy hand of the Spirit, he gives magnificent voice to the new creational power of God: the Lord has indeed remembered and has shown favour to his people. Israel, too, was about to regain its prophetic and world-changing messianic voice.

It is easy in a world of Sunday School Christmas pageants to sentimentalize and domesticate this story, confining it to cheery fireside or cozy nativity scenes. But just as John is bigger than his family—his message, like his name, will cause a disturbance whose reverberations will be felt around the world. Not even Israel will ever be the same again.

Rikk Watts
Associate Professor of New Testament,
Regent College

Psalm 80

Deliverance

*G*oing through a trial of faith seems particularly difficult during the festive, holiday season. Instead of lifting your mood, the bright Christmas lights and tinsel that mark the annual celebrations seem to jar your sensibilities. What is there to look forward to?

The lament in Psalm 80 speaks to our fallen human condition; its blueprint can be traced within our own lives.

Does this scenario sound familiar? Though you have called on God, your prayers have so far gone unanswered. Nevertheless, you petition the Shepherd once again. You echo the lament of the ancient psalmist—how long God before you come? And, like the psalmist, you are not sure just how much more that you can endure. In the psalm the Israelite reminds God of past acts of deliverance— how *Yahweh* brought the nation of Israel out of Egypt to grow as a mighty vine, only to be later ravaged by their enemies. Remembering God's past acts of grace in your own life, and his present silence, you can commiserate with the bewildered Jews. Where is God? Why is he no longer responding? Why will he not deliver me?

Hope for Jewish deliverance comes in verse 17, in the anticipation of the Messiah: "Let thy hand be upon the man of thy right hand, upon the son of man whom thou madest strong for thyself." As Christians, we can look back on the life of Jesus Christ on earth and his work on the cross. During Advent, we both celebrate our deliverance in Christ's death on the cross and anticipate his eminent return. We look forward to eternity spent in the presence of God!

Audrey Williams
Technical Services Librarian,
The John Richard Allison Library
Regent College
Regent Alum (DipCS, 2003; MCS Candidate)

Romans 1:1-7

While We Wait

*U*nknowns make me antsy—the future of the Middle East, the future of the Anglican Church, the future of my family, the future of me. A favourite friend of mine asked a counselor recently, "Why am I able to stick with a one thousand piece jigsaw puzzle, spending hours getting it completed, but can't seem to finish anything else in my entire life?" Wisely, the counselor explained, "Because you know all the pieces are there." Paul starts his introduction of the Gospel, and of himself, with the same guarantee: all the pieces of the Gospel are in place, and equally importantly, they have been from the beginning. Nothing in God's plan for his people is improvised, nothing is unpredictable, and nothing is up to us. Jesus was planned, prophesied. His lineage was organized thousands and thousands of years before Mary gave birth to him. Just when I get anxious that God really isn't in control, that the world might be falling apart as badly as it feels, Paul verifies the opposite.

And while all this predictability, this fulfilment of God's plan, comforts me and calms me down, Paul has still more to confirm: that while I wait for the planned and anticipated Messiah to come back again, I am called and beloved of Jesus. Beloved. I am worth coming for. Just when my teenagers and the computer technician look at me like I am hopeless, Paul reminds me that Jesus calls me, and loves me. Such personal love makes all this Advent waiting, all this passionate impatience, waiting now for Christmas to come, and waiting now for the Messiah to transform all the mess—bearable.

Julie Lane Gay
Vancouver, BC
Mother and Development Consultant
Regent Alum (MCS, 1983)

Psalm 97

Big God: Great Joy

ere is a paean of praise to Israel's covenant God for his awesomely wise, just and loving sovereignty, summoning us to join in.

The call to joy in the LORD's lordship opens and closes the Psalm (1, 12). This return-to-base way of rounding off a presentation is nowadays called an inclusio and pictured as bookends, linking everything in between. Joy in God's sovereignty, then, is the theme throughout.

Why should knowing that God is in total control bring joy? Because it guarantees spiritual security now and final salvation to come. Because it ensures that God's wisdom, justice, veracity and love will never fail. Because it promises a conclusive comeuppance to all forms of idolatry that enslave and distress people at present—worshipping wealth, power and privilege; idolizing self, self-service and self-satisfaction as all that matters; idealizing ideologies—capitalist, socialist, liberal, jihadist, whatever—as if they could save the world; and so on. Because it assures us that everything has meaning and value, if we can only find it, and all creative endeavours are worthwhile. So rejoice! Dwell on all this, so that your joy will flow! (There's an inclusio; did you notice?)

Advent arrives as an inclusio, looking back to Christ's first coming and on to his second and celebrating God's sovereignty in both and in everything in between. The first coming was unobtrusive: a peculiar pregnancy, a birth in a stable, and behold, the world's co-Creator had arrived within it as a human baby. Fantastic, but true! The second coming will simultaneously overwhelm everyone then alive. Also fantastic, yet also true! So, with Charles Wesley, "Rejoice in glorious hope! / Jesus the Judge shall come / And take his servants up / To their eternal home!"

And see it all in Psalm 97 terms, as sovereignty in action, for that indeed is what it is. Praise the LORD!

J. I. Packer
Board of Governors' Professor of Theology,
Regent College

Matthew 1:18-25

All in a Name!

*S*oon after arriving in rural Kenya, I awoke before dawn to a loud rapping at the door. The school matron had gone into labour and rushed for help to the headmistress as my fellow missionary's old Peugeot truck was one the few vehicles in the vicinity. Yet the nearest hospital was half an hour's drive over bumpy dirt roads, and time ran out. Overcome with birth pangs, the matron delivered her baby boy in the back of the Peugeot, and promptly named him Motokaa, the Swahili transliteration of "motorcar"!

So came my first encounter with the significance of naming children in African cultures: sometimes to mark events surrounding the child's birth, to describe the child's personality, to reflect social relationships (naming one after a relative), or to express the parents' sentiments to God (e.g., "Let God be thanked").

If parent-produced names convey such meaning, how much more significant are divinely-disclosed names? In Matthew 1:21, an angel of the LORD instructs Joseph to name Mary's Spirit-conceived child, Jesus, the Greek form of a Hebrew name meaning "*Yahweh* saves," or "God is salvation." Though a common name at the time, its designation here, the angel explains, is entirely unprecedented—"because he will save his people from their sins." Hence a single name encapsulates the totality of Jesus' mission (Lk. 4:18-21), indeed, the entire redemptive purposes of God.

Yet another name is given to Jesus: Immanuel, meaning "God with us." Citing Isaiah 7:14, Matthew indicates that the child prophesied has now come in the child born of Mary, thus fulfilling messianic expectation and bringing God's tangible presence to humanity.

So it's all in a name. Jesus. Immanuel. His identity, his import, his embodiment of the immediacy and intimacy of God's presence—his incarnation!

Diane Stinton
Nairobi, Kenya
Coordinator, MTh in African Christianity
Daystar University
Regent Alum (ThM, 1994)

46

Luke 2:1-7

Perspective

Time has a habit of altering our memories. With time comes perspective that colours the lens through which we see and recall our past. For good or for ill, when facts blur and details fade, we will remember the past in terms of the impact upon our life. And so it is that dear Luke recounts the day that God came to be with us as a baby.

But Luke, how could you forget the stories about the discomfort and weariness that Joseph and Mary (especially Mary!) experienced as they traveled to Bethlehem? How can you gloss over the angst they felt when there was no room in the inn? Confusion prevailed. Don't you remember how they asked, "Is this not the son of the most high whom we bring here in Mary's womb? If it is so, surely God would provide a place for him…and us." Luke, you've missed the depth of the story. Stay here awhile and tell it like it really happened!

Selah. Pause.

Don't we long to find ourselves in the stories we love? I often think of Mary and Joseph's experience when things don't go the way I think they should. It puts things into perspective.

And the perspective that Luke gives us, and invites us into as well, is that all things pale when compared to the immense love that God showed to us on that day. And life on earth was never to be the same from that point on.

The Advent is upon us. The waiting is drawing to a close. Emmanuel, God himself, has come to be among us. And we recall, with Luke, that all of life's issues are fallen to the side as we stop and adore this little one, our LORD and Saviour.

Brent Fearon
Cambridge, ON
Senior Program Officer, Bridgeway Foundation
Regent Alum (MCS, 1994) & former staff

John 1:1-18

He Is

*N*ow we see, on this night, at last, with these words, that it is all much more than our salvation. It is much more than a doctrine or a theology, much more than the grist for an argument about the divinity of Christ, much more than John's beautiful sentences strung together. It is not a concept or an idea, not simply a special day or a hallowed night. He is. In a way we have never seen him before. He is. A presence with weight, with toes, with breath. He is. All is caught up in that.

And his skin is my skin; my skin, his. There is nothing at all abstract about him. Or me. Where once we shared very little, now we share everything—birth, hunger, thirst, pain, laughter, death, hair and fingernails and heart. Where once there was no face for God, now there are eyes and lips and a kindness we had not always been sure of. Where once being human had meant so much fear and darkness, now we see how good it is, how brave it is, how full of light it is, because he is human, and all humanity draws its tears and hope and humanness from his.

And this face of God is also my face now, his life my life, his birth my birth, his Christmas my Christmas.

For this night I believe, and in this belief I look at my hands, whether young or old, firm or frail, and I see immortality, I see a morning rising from this night and light on these hands that is unending, because anyone who believes in the God of stables and mangers and stars and fingers, he makes a human like he is, this night he makes a child of God.

Murray Andrew Pura
Writer and Pastor
Regent Alum (DipCS 1982, ThM 1987)

Luke 2:8-20

What a Way to Save a World!

I know this story. You do too. It washes over us with assuring familiarity. Its unexpectedness no longer startles. The Advent readings in all their richness have sought to alert us that something quite unexpected will happen. We have read that "a son will be born," and that Jesus will come "in great humility." But we are still somehow unprepared for the reality of these verses. The stark vulnerability of a baby in a barn.

It is an old story; but, because some things haven't changed, it is a painfully contemporary story. The context is the complexity of Middle East politics, complete with ruthless leaders, occupied lands, war and violence, poverty and displaced people. Caught in the crush of too many people and too few resources, a young woman, and an anguishing delivery in a makeshift shelter. Not a way to save a world!

Some definitive word is needed, something to convince not just shepherds, but us, too, in our skepticism and world-weariness. And it comes! Delivered by an angel surrounded by light and glory. The text makes it clear that this baby is the focus. A baby wrapped in humanity and divinity, for he is Christ the LORD. This is the news, good news of great joy, and it is meant for all people! It is spoken in ringing angel tones and then sung by a multitude of heavenly beings. Praise soars into the cool dark air, giving glory to God for this unexpected intervention, this loving and gracious extension of peace and purpose and hope. What a way to save a world! God's way.

The shepherds respond initially with fear, but then they take the message seriously, they get caught in the joy and they rush off to find the new-born Saviour.

As I think of verse sixteen, artists, who over the years have sought to capture this moment, shape my imagination. The rough-hewn faces of the shepherds seem almost embarrassed to be intruding on the new little family, but drawn by joy and wonder, their eyes filled with amazement, they come to meet the tiny King. They see the good news and it gets hold of them, it turns them upside down, it fills them with joy! Verse twenty says, "And the shepherds returned, glorifying and praising God for all they had heard and seen." They can't wait to share it! It ripples out into their world causing wonder, but also, right from the beginning, because some things haven't changed, some respond with joy, others with jealousy.

From the drama of the angel's announcement, the surprising heavenly choir, the fear and excitement of the shepherds, the shuffling of visitors in the small stable, and the dynamic sense of spreading news, the text in verse nineteen quite suddenly shifts from external to internal, from groups and multitudes to one person. It becomes quiet, and for a brief moment we focus on Mary. "Mary kept all these things, pondering them in her heart."

We know that Mary had been given some indication of what lay ahead for her son, so she would no doubt have weighed the words of praise and declaration carefully. To ponder is perhaps another sort of wondering, but with a hint of heaviness, an awareness of shadow. Luci Shaw in her poem "Mary's Song" so poignantly expresses that shadow, when Mary says, "For him to see me mended, I must see him torn."

On Christmas Day, as we read this familiar story, may we too be caught up in the shepherds' joy. And, because some things haven't changed, may we hear and see and live out God's ways of vulnerability, humility, suffering and love.

Thena Ayres
Professor Emerita of Adult Education,
Regent College

Printed in the United States
95218LV00002B/502-1698/A